LIFE FLAME

URJANA PRITIPARNNA

ISBN 979-888569121-5

To

my parents

Contents

Contents

Contents

Acknowledgements

I may thank my parents for their constant inspiration to build my life like a flame. I must thank respected Mr.Sekhawat Ali Sir for his guidance in preparing this book. Lastly, I thank God to be present with me as unseen hand behind all achievements of my life.

Foreword

I am pleased to go through the book "Life Flame" written by Urjana Pritiparnna, a budding talent. The book is rich in tender discernments on the valuable virtues of life in a delicate manner and flair which make the poems enjoyable. I acknowledge that the tender thoughts presented in a lucid manner in this text is really praise worthy.

I wish her all success in life.

Mr.Sekhawat Ali

Prologue

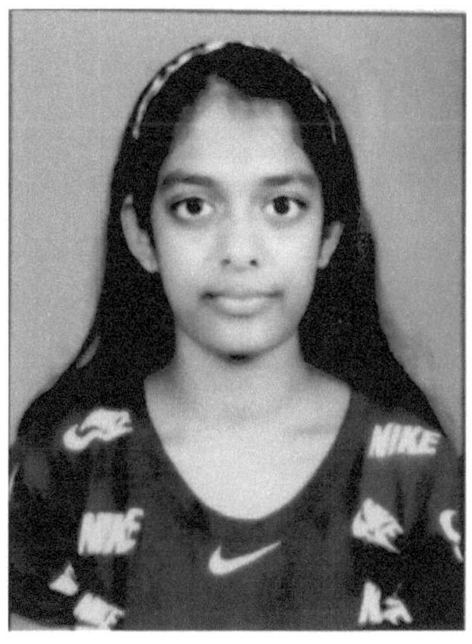

Urjana Pritiparnna

About the poet:-

Born at Baripada, Odisha (India), the young poet Urjana Pritiparnna is presently studying in Std-VII in Sri Satya Sai Vidya Vihar school, Baripada.

The poet started writing poetry at the age of 9. Most of the poetry in this book "Life Flame" were written at the age of 10 and 11. This is her first poetry collection.

The poet can be reached through urjanna2009@gmail.com

Preface

This book containing some small poems written by a budding talent like me chiefly caters to the readers the basic principles of art of leading a meaningful life. It will provide a broader scope to the readers to discover the hidden talents, to have control on anger, egotism and selfishness enabling them to deal with this toxic world. The book will also inspire the readers to discover love, fraternity, friendliness, overcoming the difficulties in life. The book is packed with priceless virtues of life that will make the readers achieve the goals of their lives if they go to the core of the enjoyable poems.

And finally the readers are earnestly requested to share their opinions for further enlightenment.

1. IN THE DARKNESS

In the dark night,
I went to the riverside
to leave all my ego
in the simplicity of a monk
as simplicity lies in spirituality.
To leave all my greed in a tree,
as tree gives everything to us
but never asks for anything.
To leave all my depression
in the flow of river
as river washes away everything.
Thus I wish to leave all my bad habits
in the darkness of the night.
To begin a new morning,
a journey with good habits.

2. DIVINE GLORY

The night was dark,
I opened my door.
When I stepped out the floor
the whole area was lit
I felt the single joy,
the single peace
and the single serene.
Suddenly I moved
towards a place where no one was present.
I saw a glory,
my feet didn't touch the land
my wings unfurled and I started flying.
Through the clouds make the moon visible.
This is the purity of divine glory.
Which gave me all the knowledge,
all the power, all the love,
all the perfection and all the harmony.
It's a wonderful night
when I found the divine inside me.

3. JOY OF THE SEVENTH HEAVEN

In the cool morning
I am playing the flute.
The tunes of the flute
vibrate into my heart.
The sleeping beauty
inside me awakens
with the touch of gentle breeze.
My thinking tickles
up to the zenith of purity
and my eyes open to infinite bliss.
Thus I feel
the pure joy of the seventh heaven.

4. THE PAST

The past is for recognising our efforts
but not to cry for them.
Because the past is past
when remembered,
looks like an autobiography.
The use of past is to recognise
your mistakes & correct them,
to let be the past the past.
To awake your aspiration
and to rewrite
your darkest days into the best days in the future.

5. LOVE

Sacrifice in love
is always desirable.
Deception in love
is always deleterious and detrimental
to your heart.
When a flower is converted
into a fruit,
the petals of the flower
have to fall.
Like that,
to form the nature of humanity,
you have to leave
all your egoism and greed.
There is no gloom in love
but everlasting glory.

6. A TURN

Never think,
your turning point
as one of the darkest days.
When a hibiscus flower fades
and falls on the ground,
A new bud is born from it.
The turning points are like this.
It may be a turn
that makes your life
Glorious or full of gloominess.

7. TRANSITION-I

After the state of difficulty and struggle
the heart is in the reddish sunset
with the depression clouds in the sky.
Turn the depressing clouds
into the calmy ones.
The reddish sunset into cool evening,
and the sombre sky
into the sky full of glittering lights.

8. TRANSITION-II

This world is an illusion
the place of darkness & anxiety.
It's not the birthday
the enjoyable & happy day
when you were as an animal
but in the form of a human.
That is the happiest day
when you are free of
all greed, egotism, suffering & expectations.
The day, when you turned
Your inside beast into a human.

9. THREE WINGS

Inside you
there are three types of wings.
The wing of aspiration,
the wing of victory,
and the wing of vital.
The wing of aspiration,
has the power
to make a ladder
towards the height.
And in each rung of it
there is strength, enthusiasm,
energy, knowledge and vitality.
Vitality is the last rung,
the seat of all powers.
After you reach
the seventh heaven
the place of victory.
Then is the wing of aspiration
that opens
all the wings to fly
with infinite freedom and joy.

10. A WALL AND A HOUSE

A wall not only separates two rooms,
separates one thing from another,
one kind of work
from another kind.
A wall separates fear from love
A wall separates depression from peace/ endurance
A wall separates doubts from consciousness
A wall separates greed from dole
A wall separates anger from harmony
And a wall of desire separates the will from poverty.
Such walls are only not visible
as the physical wall.
A house, on the other hand,
made with the same materials,
as a wall, shelters men,
any man without any distinction.

11. LIFE-I

*The life is to
blossom the flower of success
with the bud of perfection,
formed by the leaves of progress,
formed by the stem of hard work,
formed by the roots of aspiration.*

12. A FRIEND

The night is dark,
the clouds have covered the moon
at that time fireflies
show me the light.
Likewise
a friend comes near you
as a firefly
to show you light.
As breeze blows
all my depression with the wind.
As the rushing water
let's all darkness flow.
As morning appears with the rising sun
Enabling me to shed all mistakes in the darkness
and to begin with new happiness.

13. A TRUE FRIEND

A true friend is he
who rejoices your happiness
and gives you strength
in your gloomy days.
From the matty hair of Lord Shiva
the Ganga flows
and from the heart of a friend
flows endless love.
Many roses can
make a garden
but one friend can
make the world paradise.

14. THE MOON AND THE SUN

In the dark night
when the moon shines,
it gives light to everyone
yet, it has no shine of its own.
Likewise
you are the moon
and your mother is the only Sun
because of her only,
you are shining today.

15. BEYOND

Beyond the godliness
there is devotion.
Beyond worship
there is offering.
Beyond smile
there is happiness.
Beyond victory
there is courage.
Beyond the love
there is purity.
Beyond duty
there is responsibility.
And finally beyond one
there is another.

16. LORD'S GIFT

Lord gives us strength
to turn in to courage
Lord gives us work
to turn in to aspiration
Lord gives us ability
to turn in to power
Lord gives us care
to turn in to blessings.

17. LIFE-II

The life is an action.
the better you do,
the better characters you have.
The life is a garden
the more you will nourish
The more beautiful your life become.
Life is a plant the more you care
the more you will produce.

18. LIFE-III

Each part of your life
is like a raindrop.
Before it falls into the ground,
you have to catch it.
Life is a single chain bracelet
each part of it
is joined with the other,
just like that our life is,
interlocked with love,
joy, sadness and sacrifice.
Life is like the seed of a plant,
that will definitely grow
but not without
air, water and sunlight.
Your life seed will not grow
without love, sacrifice and hard work.

19. LIFE PATHS

*There are two paths
to make your life
beneficial or detrimental.
The volcano path is
the path of suffering, erotism and depression
that makes your life detrimental.
It is only the divinity
that shapes your life unto right.
Divinity doesn't mean
to worship God with uncanny devotion.
It is that,
makes your life peaceful
with the essence of spirituality.
Divinity controls the soul with in
and helps you obtain purgation.*

20. EGO AND ASPIRATION

When we wish to be
better than others
that time
ego is
born inside us.
Ego is
what spoils our talent
and undoes us.
Will a marigold ever
aspire to become a rose?
No, never is,
in nature.
Because a marigold is always a marigold
And a rose always remains a rose.
An aspiration is what
brings progress in your work
And finally,
Perfection within you
which makes you yourself and the best .
Ego spoils you

*and aspiration is what makes you
a better yourself.*

21. NOT ENOUGH

To maintain humanity
is not enough for a human.
Human life is explored
when you, be the sun for others.

22. THE WAY

The way to live is
To be sadhak.
The way to be happy is
To free of all expectations.
The way to be loved is
to give love.
The way to be harmonious is
to be always calm.
The way to find the divinity
that leads all the happiness of world is
to surrender.

23. SPECTRUM OF LIFE

Life is a spectrum
It is like a chameleon.
Sometime, makes our life
black (spiritual energy) by fire,
Sometimes green (spiritual growth) by true love,
Sometimes yellow (richness) by struggle,
Sometimes grey (symbolise ash) by wrong doing.

24. VALUE AND PRICE

There is much difference
between price and value.
The value can be achieved
from any moral activities
but price can't.
The value of yours
increases first
not the price.

25. WORRY !

Worry !
There is nothing as worry
in an evildoer.
Because he or she knows
god has given the problems
not to worry for it.
Butto realise and consider
life as water
which flows with speed & power
that it falls on a heavier stone than it.
That is the worry
that drapes us where we can nothing.

26. OLD OR ADULT

We can never say
a person is old or adult
by his grey hair & wrinkles on the face.
His grey hair indicates
the ashes of his failures
inspite of sincere efforts.
And the wrinkles on his face indicate
The signs of complacency.
He is said to be old
who has neither dream nor goal
to fulfil it, as
he thinks he has no times at all.

27. THE SWING

In a sunny morning,
I ran towards
the swing of life.
I swang there for sometimes
so low and so high that
I can even see earthworm in the grass,
sometimes so swift that
the breeze converted
into rushing wind
and sometimes.
So slow that
the flower moved much faster.
Sometimes so dark in the arbour
and sometimes so bright like the burning ball.

28. REASON

The reason
for which duty and laziness never affiliate
is courage.
The reason
for which simplicity and modesty never affiliate
is spirituality.
The reason
for which worries and inner peace never affiliate
is calmness.
The reason
for which mistakes and correctness never affiliate
is consciousness.

29. THE SUN

In the cool weather
when the sun is
behind the clouds
we all love to enjoy the time.
But, for the sun
we all exist.
We are to shine
with the power of magnanimity
like the sun in the sky.
And when we depart
everybody remember us.

30. THE MUDDLE

The moment
you step on the muddle or mud
creates ache inside you.
The environment of
the river of ego,
the clouds of failure,
take you near the darkness.
For regression is
falling into the huge
abyss of burning fire.
There is no ladder for regression
because there is the ladder for
progress & only to go up.

31. LIGHT

Light is always with you.
But you yourself are going
far from it.
Because
Light doesn't mean the end of path.
When you consider,
the conquest of a butterfly,
when he is infant, he produces
silk and in his livelihood he enjoys
the beauty of nature.
Survive is what makes us love
and happiness lies
in reaching near the light.

32. LIGHT AND DELIGHT

Light and delight,
are not the same.
Light means reaching the divine with
the purest devotion.
But delight is just
like the glaring water droplets
with the smell
of the flower's petals
falling into the grass
that makes
both grass and the flower petals
more glorious.
Light and delight
become one in two persons
whose heart are interlocked
in deep penetrating love.

33. KITE

How bright the blue sky looks
When a kite flies!
With its serpentine and flapping tail
it pleasantly flies with confidence.
But a sorrowful thing,
you could ever see,
is a kite flapping on the top of a tree.
A human is like a kite,
We must make our heart light
And open our wings
And fly in the bright sky.
To make our heart light
We must make ourselves endurant.
But a sorrowful thing
that could ever happen is that
life is not in our control.

34. VALUES

Walking along the path,
I saw a dry leaf on a tree
and a dry leaf on the ground
crunched by a person.
Then I realized
the value of love and care.
Walking along,
I saw reflections on water
and reflections on others.
Then I realized
the value of behaviour.
Walking along,
I saw a teacher with a child
and a friend with a child.
Then I realized
The value of a supporter.

35. YOUR OWN EFFORTS

The state of great joy
depends on your
sweat filled efforts.
A single drop of sweat of your own
is much more important than
a bucket of help from others.
Its like a flash of light
in the midst of deep darkness.

36. ACTION

Each and every action is carried in a fruit
and more it develops into a flower
the more you will progress
in your work.
And finally
when flower opens, you get the success.
As a fruit needs nutrients
to develop into a flower
we too need hard work
to turn our efforts in to action.

37. WHAT TO BE

One must always be peaceful
to live this life in harmony with......
leaving anger aside,
one must always be calm
to face each and every fate
with knowledge and not with confusion.
One must not be bothered
to take the right decision in every situation.

38. FRIEND: MY GUIDING ANGEL

In the sunny morning
I, with my friend
sitting in a sunflower garden
saw the bright sunflowers.
Then I thought
let me be a sunflower
and my friend be the sun
then can set up
an eternal bond of togetherness.
The next day
the morning was cool
I with my friend
sitting near a stream
saw the powerful stream
then I thought
let me be a stream
and my friend be the stone on its bed.
So, then our eternal bond never be broken.

39. ADDITION

*With strength
we can surmount all obstacles.
With offering
we can surmount all mendacity.
With trust
we can surmount all falsehood.
And with love,
all ego and egoism.*

40. ILLUSION

The whole world is an illusion,
here the love is a thorn,
impression is an ego
wealth is money,
trust is darkness.

41. REAL AUSTERITY

Your life
carries everything, good and bad,
as it were,
in a dray.
When actions are laced with austerity,
real austerity, pure and simple.
Our actions feel not
as load or burden
but as lessons and blessings of God.

42. REALIZATION

I realized that
I can't be a good friend of yours
but can be a good sister.
I realized that
I can't be a good teacher of yours
but can be a good guide.
I realized that
I can't be strength for you
but can be courage.
I realized that
I can't be joy for you
but can be a smile.

43. BE LIKE WATER

One must be like water
to have much power
to make someone peaceful.
To have much power
to flow more powerful stone from its place.
To have much power
to quench someone's thirst.
And to have much power
without which no one can exist.

44. YOUR IDENTITY

Look to this day
and feel your own character,
no human is born without an identity.
Just like a flower in bloom
spreading its aroma all around
when the smell is withered, lingering still.
Like that when we cease to exist in
your physical shape
your images and ideas
live on in other's memory.
You only have to find
your identity as
no human is born without its identity.

45. THE ATTACHMENT

Aspiration & hard work
achieve progress.
The attachment of
calmness and quietness
creates peace.
The attachment of
devotion and offering
creates grace.
The attachment of
consciousness and sincerity
creates perfection.

46. PUDDLE AND YOU

There is nothing different
between a puddle and you.
After rain,
some parts of a road
have puddle
but there is no puddle in the garden
because the roots of the plants
hold them tight.
A person is also like this.
When misfortune strikes
he fails to fight off
because of anger and grief.
He is filled with patience and endurance
he will overcome the obstacles.

47. DIVINE IN THE HEART

In a rainy area
it is sleeting,
but the frozen droplets
on the roof
are not falling down.
Our heart is
just like this.
When the calm and peace
are together
it never falls or falters
because
the divine
stays in the heart.
The wings of the heart open
when there is
Divine in the heart.

48. PATH

Path is in life
and life is in path.
It means
the way you do
that makes you achieve progress.
Without correct way
life is nothing but a mess.
Look at the plastic wrapper
wrapped around books,
when we tear
it looks more beautiful.
And it is because
wrapper prevents dust.
Like wise
the real beauty of hard work
lies in unleashing
the visible success you achieve.

49. ANGER

Life is like a circle
and each part of it
is connected with happiness,
but very sad part is
you who destroy it.
Look to the fiery volcano,
destroying people
by its fast-moving lavas.
Like wise
your fiery anger
destroying your peace and happiness
by its destructive sparks.

50. MY MOTHERLAND

After the storm stopped,

I went outside

to make the apex clouds composure,

to make the rushing wind the breeze

and to make the shining sun visible.

After this

the sweet fresh fruits made me hungry

and my happiness becomes twice

by the smell of my motherland.

This is my motherland India.